THE EGG

Created by Gallimard Jeunesse
and Pascale de Bourgoing
Illustrated by René Mettler

A FIRST DISCOVERY BOOK

Cartwheel
·B·O·O·K·S·®

SCHOLASTIC INC.

New York   Toronto   London   Auckland   Sydney

Inside the shell
is the golden yolk,
surrounded by the white.

Here is an egg.
Let's look inside!

Most of the eggs
we eat come from chickens.
But nearly all animals produce eggs.

An egg is formed
inside a hen.

A hen is a
female chicken.
A rooster is a male chicken.
The rooster and hen must mate
to create a baby chick.

The hen sits on her eggs
to keep them warm.
Inside the shell, a chick is
starting to form.
The white and the yolk will
nourish the chick until it hatches.

The hen spends
most of her time on
the nest until
the chicks are born.

The hard shell protects the chick.

After only two days,
the chick is beginning to form.

It grows quickly. In twenty-one days,
it will be ready to hatch.

Watch!
The shell cracks.
The chick breaks through
with its sharp little beak.

A
chick
is born!

In a few
hours,
it can eat
and walk
by itself.

All these other farmyard fowl lay eggs, too.

Turkey

Ducks

Guinea hen

Pigeons

These females
sit on their eggs
until they hatch,
just as hens do.

Goose and goslings

Swallow

Robin

Crow

Blackbird

Birds in the wild
also lay eggs. These eggs are all different
sizes and colors.

Owl

The ostrich's egg is
almost as big as this book!
It is the biggest egg of all.

Ostrich

The shell
of the snake egg
expands as the
young snake grows.

Did you know that reptiles lay eggs, too?

The turtle
buries her eggs.
She doesn't sit on them.

Most reptiles are born in the summer.
The heat warms the eggs, helping them to hatch.

At birth, baby
crocodiles look just
like their mother.

Dragonfly

Ladybug eggs

Louse

Spider

Many other
kinds of animals
also lay eggs.

Frog

Ants

Mosquito   Butterfly   Slug   Lizard

The snail lays its eggs
in a hole in the ground.

Cod

This cod's ovary
contains millions of eggs.

Flying fish

Many fish lay
thousands of eggs
at once.

Ray

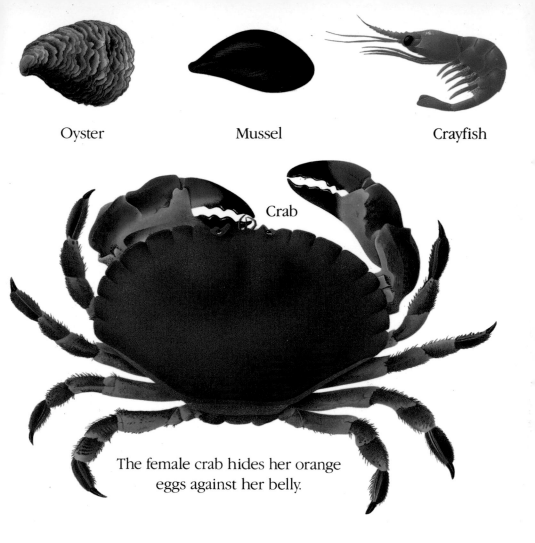

Oyster

Mussel

Crayfish

Crab

The female crab hides her orange eggs against her belly.

Shellfish and crustaceans lay eggs, too.

Fried eggs   Caviar   Salmon eggs   Hard-boiled eggs

Soft-boiled egg in a cup

What kind of eggs do you like to eat?

Titles in the series of *First Discovery Books:*

Airplanes
  and Flying Machines
Bears
Birds
Winner, 1993
Parents Magazine
"Best Books" Award
Boats
Winner, 1993
Parents Magazine
"Best Books" Award
The Camera
Winner, 1993
Parents Magazine
"Best Books" Award
Castles
Winner, 1993
Parents Magazine
"Best Books" Award

Cats
Colors
Dinosaurs
The Earth and Sky
The Egg
Winner, 1992
Parenting Magazine
Reading Magic Award
Flowers
Fruit
The Ladybug and
  Other Insects
Light
Musical Instruments
The Rain Forest
The River
Winner, 1993
Parents Magazine
"Best Books" Award

The Tree
Winner, 1992
Parenting Magazine
Reading Magic Award
Vegetables in the
  Garden
Weather
Winner
Oppenheim Toy Portfolio
Gold Seal Award
Whales
Winner, 1993
Parents Magazine
"Best Books" Award

Library of Congress Cataloging-in-Publication Data available.
Originally published in France under the title *L'œuf* by Editions Gallimard.

ISBN 0-590-45266-5
Copyright © 1989 by Editions Gallimard.

This edition English translation by Karen Backstein.
This edition American text by Louise Goldsen.
All rights reserved. First published in the U.S.A. in 1992
by Scholastic Inc., by arrangement with Editions Gallimard.
CARTWHEEL BOOKS is a registered trademark of Scholastic Inc.
13 12 11 10 9   5 6 7 8 9/9
Printed in Italy by Editoriale Libraria
First Scholastic printing, March 1992

And what about
chocolate eggs?